Rich Sibling
Poor Sibling

How Does One Sibling Become Rich, and the Other Poor?

Maura Ikharo

To the love of my life, Jibril A. Ikharo,
an exceptional linguist and the best husband and friend in
the world. I'm grateful to have you as my partner in life.

~~~~~~~~~~~~~

To everyone who loves and supports me.

And,

To everyone who loves…
~~~~~~~~~~~~~

Contents

Introduction: Rich Sibling Poor Sibling

If you have siblings, you know that people born in the same family can be completely different. Those differences become drastic when one sibling is rich and the other is poor. As the wealth gap widens between classes, it hits hardest at home. It's easy to say that the guy speeding off in a Ferrari after brunch got rich from luck when you don't have the same parents. The girl showcasing her luxury travel pictures, as she jets from one continent to the next, makes sense when you assume her father was an oil tycoon and not your dad. But what happens when you can travel the world at your leisure, yet your siblings don't even have a passport? What happens when you're touring potential real estate investments for future tenants, but your siblings are living in government-subsidized housing? That's my life. And your family may look like mine. Get ready for a whirlwind in every chapter!

If you grew up poor or middle class, like me, the trajectory of your entire life can shift based on the opportunities you take or miss early in life. That's because one opportunity often leads to another. Therefore, if you miss an opportunity early on, you may not get another shot, but if you take it, the world continues to open up to you. This is easiest to see when comparing siblings because siblings are the closest thing we have to a level playing field. We share DNA, were raised with the same household income, in the same community, have the same parent(s), and usually attend the same schools, even if one of us is a bit older or younger. We also have most of the same early opportunities or a shared lack of access to certain opportunities. But at no point are we the same because our natures are inherently different, the way we spend our time is increasingly different, and most parents treat each child differently, whether it's fair or not. I was not the preferred child, and we'll have the old, "Nature vs Nurture" debate later in the book. I'll save you some time: nature, combined with what you are exposed to, and the nurture of your peers (not your parents), plays a large role in who we become as a whole.

Let's get down to the money. If your parents were working class, we have something in common. If you knew you wanted more wealth for your future self and legacy, and still want more, this is your book. I wrote this for us. I kept the book short because I know we're on the move.

I went out and got what I wanted, despite most things in my childhood environment reflecting lack. I wrote this because I've always had people ask me how my siblings and I were raised in the same home though we led contrasting lives. Because of those questions, I closely examined potential reasons for our differences throughout our lives. You've probably contemplated the differences in your own family.

I was the eldest of three children: two girls and a boy, in that order. Our father worked insane hours in an auto factory in Metro Detroit, Michigan, while our mother worked varying shifts managing a grocery store. While many people in our community thought of those as secure jobs that positioned us in the middle-class, our parents could've been fired or laid off at any time. Both of them faced that harsh reality daily. They didn't wake up excited to go to work, they just did what they had to do, and that's what I love about the working-class spirit. That grind is honorable. However, all of that back-breaking work is for someone else's company, in hopes that you and yours will have a little stability while you're alive.

One disagreement with a bad boss can be the end. One pandemic or economic recession can mean the end of your job too. While this book isn't about quitting your job, it is about encouraging you to make sure you have various streams of income and leverage the job(s) you work to expand your assets. From there, you can leave if and when you want. When you have assets, your money works for you. When you have liabilities, you work to pay for them, and they lose value (depreciate). Robert Kiyosaki's book, Rich Dad, Poor Dad, does an amazing job explaining rich lessons in money and is recommended reading. If you're rich and concerned about how to pass on long-term generational wealth, I recommend Family

Wealth, by James E. Hughes Jr. But what happens when you have financial literacy, but the people close to you (your family: siblings, parents) do not, and may have little to no interest in it? Welcome to an oft-overlooked familial wealth gap.

I never wanted to live under the threat of financial instability and was determined to change things. I'm sure you don't want to live a life worried about being let go from your only source of income either, nor do my siblings. I've always told myself that no one else was my boss or my manager. We all need the discipline to manage ourselves. The determination to change my circumstances, and execute on that vision, is what made the difference in my life. Execution is make or break. Rich people get richer because they become marksmen. The more you practice, the more you hit your targets. Therefore, anyone skilled in accomplishing goals only gets better with time. You may fail repeatedly in the beginning, but if you keep rising to the challenge, you'll stand in the end.

The things that used to take a lot of time and energy, will become easier. You'll realize what you need to spend time on, and what you should delegate to others. Most schools don't teach anything about wealth, but high school economics taught me about specialization and division of labor. In short, you shouldn't do everything! It's not because you can't because you absolutely can try, and many small business owners do just that. The problem is that when you try to do everything, you produce lower results across the board. It's the same reason why raising children alone is hard as hell. You will stretch yourself too thin and ultimately miss some things. It takes a village to raise a child, just like it takes a village to raise a business, or a community. Sure, one self-made person can get started alone, but scaling up requires a team.

Many people get stuck running in a loop, yet still think they're making progress towards success or wealth because they're exhausted and busy all the time. It doesn't matter if they work two or three jobs, they're still stuck. Every year, they wonder why they're in the same place as last year, or worse off. It's because they're not laser-focused on what they do best. Do what you do best and strengthen those areas. Find other great people to cover the other areas. That's specialization. You should still learn as much as possible, but when you aim, aim at one thing at a time. That's why a sharpshooter doesn't miss the target. You don't need to make the gun and mold the bullets, even if you know how to do it. You just need to hit your target!

If you haven't guessed by now, I'm the rich sibling. I'm not perfect, and as I said, I wasn't even the favorite child—my mother only wanted a boy, and I was reminded numerous times. Nor was I born with an advantage over my able-bodied siblings. We have the same parents, but we've always been different because people are different. But there's more to the story. I was the nerdy sibling who no one wanted to hear from until checks started rolling in and my life looked unfamiliar to poverty. Maybe this happened to you too. At first, I was considered weird for using paychecks from my job to invest in myself and assets, instead of liabilities, like flashy clothing and depreciating cars.

My siblings spent money like it had an expiration date and wondered why I didn't do the same. After all, it's how we were raised. If you've got it, flaunt it, or no one will know you have it. That's not sound advice. I don't look rich, I live it. And you should too. There's nothing you can buy that compares to freedom and options. That's why people die for it every day around the world. When you've tasted real freedom, it's hard to go back to a life without it.

As a child, when I talked about wanting wealth in various areas of my life, it was met with disdain. You probably know what I'm talking about. Most people in my family would tell me that I thought that I was better than them. "Money is the root of all evil," they'd say. But that's a common Biblical misquote. It's actually, "The love of money is the root of all evil." And I never loved money; I've always loved freedom and options. Money, used as the tool it is, allowed me to buy back my freedom and more options. It'll do the same for you if it hasn't already. I didn't stumble into wealth one day on my way to work. No one ever gave me thousands of dollars to get a jump start on life, yet I get asked to provide it all the time by people who wouldn't otherwise mention my name. Wealth is a long game and takes time and patience. I'm just getting started! You will see throughout this book, that our differences reflect the way we spend our time, not just our money.

As a kid, I thought wealth happened fast. I didn't know shit about real wealth. I thought money came quickly from gambling and was meant to spend just as fast. Winning the lottery was a dream for my family. Every year we'd win hundreds to a couple of thousand dollars at once, but it didn't compare to how much was lost buying tickets every day. I didn't know that then. I just knew my family was happy when money came in and was irritable when it was gone.

I used to watch the lottery with them every night, hoping for another win. Winning money felt good. Big money! Crisp new bills made my hand tingle in anticipation of buying something new. The elders in my family would sometimes send me to the local corner store to play the lottery for them when I was seven or eight years old. I remember seeing hopeful lucky numbers written on nearly every loose sheet of paper in the house, from mail envelopes to the back of old homework assignments. For us, the lottery was how big money was made. Instant gratification was golden. To be rich, I believed you either had to hit the lottery, win on a television game show, get a payout from insurance after a loved one's death, or you were just born rich. Regardless, chance was involved in wealth, not work. You couldn't just tell my family that hard work made people rich because my family already worked hard, yet knew they'd never be rich unless they were lucky. Something big had to happen.

But I didn't get lucky. I got tired of crazy shit happening around me. My father died from drugs. My brother is serving his sentence in a level five prison (that's maximum). Both of those phone calls came unexpectedly. Over the years, I was nearly desensitized to abuse and drama because it was so commonplace in my family. I expected it. Though we were raised together, my brother went to prison, and my sister works shifts in the fast-food industry. Neither wants to be where they are. My siblings earn less than our parents, even when considering each parent individually. They've dropped from our parents' middle-class income, into poverty. I earn more than my parents did. We're examples of the fleeting middle-class. The rich and poor are both growing, as the middle dwindles. None of our outcomes happened overnight. If you're from a family of stark contrasts, you know this. If not, we'll get you caught up.

I faced shock, embarrassment and shame throughout my early years because I was different. Because I wanted something else. I didn't know how to deal with being seen as unusual by my family, in a place that was supposed to be my home. For example, my family would teasingly tell me I was adopted whenever they saw me reading because reading was a strange hobby. Many people we knew stopped reading in high school, so leisure reading was unheard of.

I did the only thing I could as an adolescent; I found other environments to be in during the day and stretched as many of those days into my nights as I could. This was the beginning of shifting the way I spent my time. I'd spend extra hours at softball or volleyball practice working out, tutoring students after school, catching up with friends, or at the library. It was important for me to expose myself to people who wanted the same things as I did and encouraged me to be my best. I loved being surrounded by peace and encouragement and found a new inner circle, and a new home in them. When I talk about wealth and being the rich sibling in this book, it's about much more than money, though money is an important tool.

I wonder how many people have family members as the first barrier of entry to new environments and wealth. The family shouldn't be an obstacle for children or adults to overcome. Don't ever try to block someone else's vision because you can't see it. You didn't see it because it wasn't for you. And never allow anyone to discourage or belittle you because of their fears, envy, or whatever it is. We shouldn't take those things to heart because we all have our legacies to fulfill before our time is up. I spent my life losing people I loved, so I want to leave something for the ones who come after me, and the ones who've battled beside me in the trenches.

If you've ever been the black sheep of your family for doing something good, I'm proud of you. Keep pushing forward. When you arrive at the right pasture for you, all of the sheep will be black too.

Welcome home! I love y'all!

Chapter 1: How the Hell Did You Become the Rich Sibling?

Becoming the "rich sibling" can happen in any number of ways, but this was the sequence that kicked the door to wealth open for me. Before we go there, you should know that wealth is far beyond money. Being the rich sibling isn't just financial; it's also a wealth of great relationships, including an amazing spouse, good health, and a strong spirit. It's a wealth of faith. These were my steps to wealth:

1. Exposure
This is being exposed to an environment or situation (good or bad) that sparks an initial vision in you.

2. Vision
These are the images and feelings of what you know life should be for you.

3. Re-exposure
Confirmation that your vision can be accomplished. You've either seen it somewhere, heard it or read about it.

4. Drive
The willpower and faith to accomplish your vision.

5. Execution
Doing what needs to be done and achieving your vision.

Exposure

We are constantly exposed to things every day. As adults, we have more control over our exposure, but as children, our parents and elders dominate what we hear and see, and often how we react to what we feel. If you take nothing else from this book, remember that exposure is the most important variable in the outcome. That's because the things you execute on, good or bad, depend on what you've been exposed to.

My siblings and I were often exposed to hyper-sexual, violent, R-Rated films and experiences as children. Scenes of domestic violence, sex, and other abuse played before our eyes daily. We saw our father strung out from drugs, and we later saw him dead in the emergency room from that drug abuse. This is no disrespect to my loving father who always encouraged us to be our best selves and showed up to help out at my softball practices. These are just the hard facts of my life. Fighting and trash talk in school and the streets were encouraged by our family. If someone said something about you or hit you, you were supposed to handle that person immediately. Reporting it to a teacher was considered being a tattletale, and snitches get stitches. Due to that exposure, I choked a girl in kindergarten when she made a joke about my dad. I tackled a boy when he teased one of my friends during recess in second grade. I didn't care about the consequences because

I'd already received permission from my parents to kick some ass. My siblings were no different from me. My sister was expelled from our school district in high school for beating a kid in the head with her heel shoe after the fight was over. My brother fought his neighborhood friends and dropped out of school entirely. He stopped attending regularly in middle school. This is not rocket science, but some people will say they never would've imagined a negative outcome from their children or themselves, though they usually submerged their kids in negativity. It's all they were exposed to!

In my environment, education wasn't important. Several wealthy college dropouts will tell you that going to college is a waste of time, and most [public] schools in the U.S. only teach kids how to be poor employees. I'm not debating any of that. However, those same people will also tell you that education itself is vital. This chapter is not about college or your country's school system, it's about the fundamentals of knowledge. I don't know a bunch of rich people who didn't go to college. I know a ton of poor people who didn't. The majority of the people with money in my life, pursued higher education, regardless of whether they found it useful. The things I learned in college about wealth were not taught in the classroom. However, college at an elite university exposed me to wealthy peers.

I was not taught to value education at home. Learning was an afterthought. Reading and finances were nothing more than assignments. I fully believe that high school dropouts can be as successful as those who graduated high school, college or beyond. However, you will not gain wealth or run a successful business or life without knowledge. Education, in this book, is about exposure to the financial literacy and mindset that many people never learn or see. It's about how financial knowledge creates immense wealth gaps, even in families, all the way down to the siblings who shared a roof and lineage. I took the energy I spent fighting in the schoolyard and turned it towards the bank. I changed my mindset and the way I spent my time.

In the early years of my childhood, I was not learning much in school. I thought all schools ended in 6th grade because that was the last level of my elementary school and no one ever spoke to me about life beyond that. That means, I thought 12-year-olds were done with schooling. I had older cousins, but we didn't talk about school together. We fought, raced and played games. I was in 4th or 5th grade when I found out about junior high school and high school, and still knew nothing about college. While there were shows on TV featuring college students, I didn't understand the setting because college was a foreign concept. It was like hearing a word in a different language; I knew it meant something to someone, but it meant nothing to me.

My grandparents didn't finish elementary school, so my parents graduating from high school were a success. They didn't have to consider college, because they'd already made progress and jobs were readily available. My mother thought about becoming a nurse and attended community college for a bit when we were kids, before leaving without the support to stay. My parents got jobs with pensions, and that was the dream. Or at least, that's the dream they were exposed to having, and the dream they exposed us to as well.

I remember being laughed at by my junior high school counselors when I told them my goal was to get "Straight As" in my first semester there. I didn't have a successful record. My elementary school grades sucked; I'd been to detention for fighting at two different schools and had no track record of consistently good performance. But I knew I was getting better. And even if they doubted my abilities, they should've encouraged me and referred me to the resources that could help me. I took their laughter with a grain of salt and set out to achieve my goal. I love a challenge and succeeded in getting "Straight As". Here's the thing—I was a smart student who scored high in all standardized tests, but usually performed at a D or C-level in school because I rarely did homework. No one was asking about schoolwork when I got home. My parents were at work, and when they came home, my job was to make sure the house was clean. If the house wasn't spotless, I was getting a beating. Therefore, I didn't have fears about failing a test, my fear was about being beaten. I didn't see the rod of discipline and guidance, only the rod of control. My parents weren't different from their parents, or the parents of most of the kids in our community. They weren't monsters; it's just what they knew and experienced. The school wasn't going to provide for our future families, we'd have to go through a boss, or higher ranks in the military, and needed to know how to obey authority. No explanation makes it right, but I understand the roots. Some of it comes from the mindset of striking a child before life strikes them harder. The rest of it is from generations of subservient roles where laborers were flogged for disobeying orders like cleaning up or tending to things faster. That training was passed down for centuries. I know this because we never aged out of being hit, unlike some other kids in the community. You were never too old for your parents to strike you, even if you had children of your own. That's problematic to say the least.

I hated living like that. Reading expanded my world, but it was hard to read while surrounded by a cacophony of altercations. There were kids in my elementary classes that lived peaceful lives, went to Hawaii for spring breaks, and some wore bathing suits under their clothes because they had swimming pools in their backyards. Having a pool was a big deal in Michigan because it's cold as hell (it burns), so warm days spent poolside or at the lake were cherished. It was rare to know a family with a real, inground pool where I'm from. When you're poor, having your own house, your own room, AND a pool was seen as an extreme luxury, especially in the eyes of a child. I heard about the pool parties at school, but I never got invited because I wasn't considered to be a good kid from a good family. That sounds harsh, but this is what true stories sound like for the poor. Those students weren't mean to me directly, or negative, but I was mean to them because it's all I knew. I wanted to hang out with them, but I couldn't, and I knew it. My nephew is just a kid, as I write this, but he knows he's poor. He told me that he doesn't have any friends, and I know how he feels because he attends my old elementary school. Any school will do. It's interesting how poor kids know their poor early on, but I've heard stories from some of my rich friends saying they didn't know they were rich until they were older. Life was just normal to them. Disharmony never feels right, and children with peaceful lives almost instinctively turn away from us.

That exposure taught me about being locked out of a network, not just because of money, but because of mentality. The way I acted (i.e., fighting, bullying), made the kids uncomfortable, and their parents assumed that it's how I was being raised. They were correct. Making jokes about people was how my family and friends spoke to one another, but it didn't work in the environment I wanted to be in. Sure, rich jerks exist, but they weren't attending my school.

Though I didn't see the pools of my peers, I knew they were having fun in them and feeling like free kids. I saw their parents helping out at our school. Those parents came on field trips and bought cool gifts for their kids and friends at museum gift shops. I always wished my parents could be there. I wished I had a few dollars to get something from the gift shops too. Or a few dollars to buy a lunch that wasn't soggy in my paper bag. I remember when some other poor friends and I would put our loose coins together at the Boys and Girls Club to buy a burrito or slice of pizza to share. We'd do the same after volleyball and softball night games when we got to junior high. It's no wonder I got a job before high school.

I saw how happy some of my peers were and I wanted to be happier. I knew I wanted to have time to be there for my kids in the future. My friends and I still had a great time, but we knew we were poor and that some kids still had it much worse than us. I had a house to go home to, while some friends were living with ten to fifteen people in an apartment.

While we're on that, I'd be remiss if I did not say that my family took me and my siblings on vacation. We had a lot of fun. My maternal family lived in Florida, so the five of us would pile up in our van and listen to Motown albums for over 1,000 miles on the road from Romulus, Michigan to Orlando, Florida. We'd stay in a villa-style hotel in Kissimmee, not far from Disney World and Universal Studios, and hang out in that area. My parents got a special price because they said they wanted a timeshare, and in exchange, had to sit through a long, aggressive sales pitch. Timeshares are scams because you're never finished paying due to rising maintenance fees, and sometimes you can't go when you want, depending on the contract. Anyway, we never went to Disney World as a family because it was too expensive for five people. However, one of my uncles had extra tickets from his trip (also a family of five), so we were able to go to Universal Studios and SeaWorld. Back then, extra days on tickets didn't expire, so people would resell them or give them away. I'm so grateful for those experiences because that's how I knew I wanted to travel. Learning about different countries in school also sparked my interest, but seeing new places changed everything.

What were you exposed to as a child? What are you exposing yourself or your children to now?

Vision

Step two is having a vision. Everyone has a vision. Your initial vision is largely based on what you've been exposed to, good or bad. While I was exposed to many negative things and would've envisioned that for my future, I saw positive options that spoke to my spirit. I challenge you to think big. Get crazy with it! My vision has changed over the years, but originally, it was straight-forward. I just wanted to travel, be happy and have a peaceful family. By the end of high school, I wanted to have a happy, drug-free, and drama-free family; travel the world; attend the University of Michigan (Go Blue!); live in the best areas (with multiple homes); drive a luxury car (and be driven); have a healthy body, and have the freedom to do whatever I wanted as an adult. My vision was a world away from what my siblings and I knew.

What is your vision? Write it down. If you can write it, you can make it real.

____

____

____

____

____

____

____

____

____

____

____

____

____

____

____

____

———————————————————————

———————————————————————

———————————————————————

———————————————————————

———————————————————————

If you're visual, like me, use the rest of this space to illustrate your vision:

Never let someone else's fears block your vision. I don't care if you're still living with your parents, or have children of your own at home. If you have a vision, you have the right to it. Go get that shit! People in my household told me not to pursue certain things because it sounded too difficult and they didn't want me to fail. Failing is good! Failure is simply a process of elimination. You figure out better methods of achieving the goal through the elimination process we call "failure". I'm almost always better in the second take than in the first. If you haven't failed, you haven't taken any real risks towards success. I did what I had to do and, in the end, and I made it.

Step one of my vision was to move out of my parents' house and into my dream college. Do you need to go to college to be rich? No! There are a ton of successful people who didn't graduate from college. Some are famous! College was just my way out, and I knew it. It allowed me to pack my bags and get out. Some folks have the luxury of a welcoming family, but we were hurried to become adults. I knew people who went to college with me and quit because they were spending too much time back home in our neighborhood during the week and on weekends. The environment we came from is not the place to return to while you're trying to progress. This is not meant to be disrespectful. Professional athletes [who win] don't hang out all day, they practice and hit the gym. Students should be in the library (or wherever you learn), studying abroad, and interning around the world.

If you're a student reading this, and you don't have multiple streams of income lined up or an internship that can help bank you one day, you shouldn't be out partying, unless it pays you. I almost threw my life away hanging out because I had imposter syndrome and felt like I didn't belong in school. Yes, students party, but they also go to class. I was not in class. A party is a celebration or marketing for a brand. What are you celebrating if you're struggling? What are you marketing if you don't own it? If you're not a student, and you're out partying, or binge-watching shows and movies every day, without pay, the same rules apply. You will never get those hours back. Time is the greatest asset and luxury of the rich.

I get it. Sometimes things are hard, and you want to let loose a bit. Take care of your mental health. I'm not telling you to neglect yourself, but the biggest self-neglect is ignoring your vision. You're ignoring who you should be. It doesn't benefit you or anyone else to forgo who you should be, to be a shell of yourself, or worse, trying to be someone else, or who they envision you to be.

There were economic opportunities in college that I passed up because I was too hungover to execute. My vision didn't matter because my mind was cloudy. My father passing during my junior year in college was my wake-up call. I was blowing an opportunity that he never had, and that he was immensely proud of me for before he died. On top of that, he was never going to be alive to support me again. I knew there was no one left to support me financially, but me. My brother had already dropped out of high school, and my sister was trying to graduate in an alternative high school program. There was no home for me to return to. I got my grades together and started thinking about what my next moves would be after college. I graduated with nothing but a piece of paper saying I'd finished, and the fortunate opportunity to have been re-exposed to more while I was there.

Re-Exposure

Remember the kids from my elementary school (or yours) with the swimming pools in their backyards and holidays in Hawaii? Well, college at an elite university was far beyond that. It showed me that my whole community was working-class, and middle class at best. This was the re-exposure to a world that I knew existed, but not at this level. There were kids parking Maseratis carelessly around campus, without regard for law enforcement. Runway-ready girls were packed in Range Rovers to travel a few blocks to fraternity row. Students were making their first political decisions based on their parents' high incomes and tax brackets. I had a classmate in my first semester with an orchard in her backyard, and she wasn't the only classmate I met with an orchard. Students were having conversations I'd never heard. My parents and siblings hadn't heard anything like this either, yet there I was, soaking it up. I felt like an imposter, but I was also intrigued to listen in on moneyed conversations.

The house I grew up in was less than 2,000 square feet, which was possibly the size of one of my classmate's gatehouses. That's where the guards maintain the entry gate and may sleep depending on the setup. Those students had bedrooms bigger than my house or several of my houses together. These were the houses with driveways that went on for miles off the road and were hidden from mapping platforms for security. I listened to these conversations in our cafeterias, libraries, and during group projects, as they talked about where they "summered", as well as where they escaped to for winter. I was excited, never envious, and wanted to know more about that life.

I listened intently and tried not to give too much information away about my own life. Eventually I overcame my unwarranted shame, and embraced my full journey, but at the time, I didn't want to risk being shut out of conversations like I'd been when I was younger. Their families took trips to the Olympics, Italy, and Paris for fashion, and to South America for its history. These were common gifts from parents for birthdays and graduations. I didn't even have a passport in college, unlike my spouse, who grew up with two! I didn't know the steps to getting a passport either, although one of my visions was to travel the world. Ha! That takes me to my next vision point: preparation.

If your vision is to travel, get a passport. Mileage may vary in your country, but in the USA and UK, passports are valid for 10 years. In Nigeria, they're good for 5 years. Maybe you don't have the money to travel today but get a passport to prepare yourself to go. There are little things you can do to start tasting the future and creating an environment of re-exposure. If you want a mansion, go to open houses for them. Test drive that luxury vehicle at the dealership for free! You need to feel it, touch it, taste it. Life isn't about obtaining things, but that doesn't mean you can't have what you want. If you have a flight (especially domestic), and the upgrade to first class is something you can afford (even if just barely), upgrade your seat! If your job reimburses you for flights, at least pay for the upgrade yourself. You need to expose yourself to the next level. You won't want to go back, but you'll have something to keep working towards. And don't give me the excuse of not wanting to spoil yourself to the point where you can't appreciate the little things. Be you but be the best you possible. Trust me, you will be a better you with exceptional service and phenomenal sleep, than with rude people and subpar accommodations. The importance of exposure cannot be overstated. It made the list twice for a reason! The first time you're exposed, it may come upon you without you seeking it out. "Re-exposure" is all about you taking control of your life and seeking something new. If you don't seek for yourself, something else will seek and find you.

Re-exposure doesn't mean spending beyond your means or "fake it until you make it." I knew what I wanted, so I read about it, watched videos, went to networking events and moved out of my home state. You may have to move to meet your opportunity! Maybe your opportunity hasn't knocked at your door because you're in the wrong house. After I relocated, I was only making $975 per month, while paying $500 for rent, on top of food and car insurance. More than half of my income went to housing and I hadn't eaten yet. I went to college (barely made it out), and still didn't have my vision, but I was working on it. I instinctively felt like I was on the right path, and I was. Listen to your gut. If your gut is always steering you wrong, you need to train it! I saved my scraps and hustled when I could to make a few extra dollars to get me in a better environment. I was uncomfortable showing up to opportunities driving in my hooptie car at first, but I held my head up and stepped out like it was a Bentley because at least I had access to a vehicle and a brighter future.

When you get in the next level environment, pay attention to your surroundings. What are people doing? What do they look like, sound like, act like? You don't have to imitate anyone, and shouldn't, but you do need to become familiar with where you want to be. Know who you're talking to and know who you are. Do your research and keep yourself apprised of the happenings in the community you want to be in. Don't just be yourself—be your best self!

Being an avid reader was always my ticket to next-level thinking. I read all of the pedigree-based, upward social mobility, and financial literacy books I could get my hands on. I wanted to prepare my mind for change. I watched movies set in private schools, on Wall Street, or in high fashion, but I never assumed the people would be anything like the movies or books because of creative freedom. It was just fun! I thought about the opportunities I could provide my children due to my exposure. It was all about seeing a life I didn't have access to in-person and wanting more than just a glimpse. I wanted a shot at being footloose and fancy-free. I dreamed of the day I'd be jetting off to France at the drop of a hat, then down to Kenya for a private safari, and finally unwinding in luxury spa after a day in the bush. I experienced that exciting trip spread across two continents and the child in me is still glowing inside. Kenya is one of the best places in the world in terms of culture, climate, wildlife, food, and luxury, and will always have a place in my heart. I love all of Africa and have a family home in Nigeria. None of these luxuries came into fruition until the execution phase, but the re-exposure step led me to that point. And as I explore the world, new cultures and languages, I'm repeatedly exposed to more.

Exposure is powerful! Re-exposure is your opportunity to take control of what you're exposed to. It's an opportunity to change your narrative instead of living what was written.

What are some things you're working to get exposed to? Which great experiences have you already exposed yourself to?

____

____

____

____

____

____

____

____

____

____

____

____

____

____

____

____

Drive

After all of the exposure and vision, you still have to want to take action and begin. This will be a short section because you either have the drive or you don't. Think about a vehicle. If you put it in "Drive" and take your foot off of the brake, it will probably move a little bit, but it's not going far. If you're parked on a hill, a car in "Drive" won't move forward at all unless you accelerate. That's life. You can put yourself in "Drive" mode, and take your foot off the brake, but until you hit the gas, you're stagnant. Some people think they're moving forward, but as soon as they get to a hill (read: obstacle), they can't overcome it because they never hit the gas. They were operating under the facade of "Drive" mode but doing little more than idling. Drive requires hitting the gas, and the courage to go. Drive also requires buying gas and access to a vehicle. That's preparation. Drive is all about gearing up and setting out to a destination. The destination is your vision. Nothing compares 100% to life, so no analogy will be exactly like your experience. The point is, you have to work at your vision to achieve it. You have to want to go and go.

The other thing about drive, is the directionality of it. You need a plan for your vision. It's not enough just to see it and want it. Think about how you're going to get there, potential paths, and how long it could take along the worst paths and life detours. We must be flexible, yet always heading toward the destination, or rerouting to get there. Ambition is one of those things that we have in our nature. It's what separates the people who only talk about their visions, from those who achieve them. I could've stopped at "re-exposure" and went on living knowing that there was a better life for me possible out there. I could've told myself that I could find happiness without that other life. For me, that wouldn't have been true because I can't be happy knowing I'm not doing everything to achieve the things I know I can, and also the life beyond my imagination. I'm not content as a bystander in my own life. This book wasn't written for bystanders. I write for those willing to act. Show the world what's possible! As we say in faith, "Let Him use you!"

Even if you don't believe, go be of service and let someone know they can be great.

Execution

Execution is tricky because you can work all day and night until your back breaks, but still, never execute. There's a misconception that working hard is execution. Execution is the end of something. It means an objective was carried out to completion. If the results don't hit the target, there was no execution. For example, if you want to be a real estate investor, you don't need to take courses to become a real estate agent or broker. You'd spend countless hours taking classes and studying for exams, only to learn that you're still not an investor, even after you pass the test. I've met people who say they haven't bought properties for themselves because they aren't agents. Becoming an agent in the USA is not what it takes to execute on investing in a property for yourself. You just need the money or leverage to buy the property, and to close the deal. Real estate is still one of the best forms of investment for two reasons: 1) everyone needs a place to live as a basic necessity; and 2) you're already in real estate—you either own the property, or you're renting it from an owner. Get on the right side of finances. You're either a consumer or a producer. We live in a consumer society. Nearly everything is a commodity. Make sure you're producing and gaining assets, not liabilities. A house is a liability if you're not getting paid for it. Make sure someone is paying you and therefore putting more equity into the property and money in your pocket. From there, you can refinance the home, and use the equity from your tenant's rent payments to purchase more properties. That's how you become a rich sibling! It's not what you spend, it's what you keep, and how you use what you have.

I don't know if my initial vision was entirely different from my poor siblings, but I know that my re-exposure was different, I had drive, and I executed on what I wanted. I didn't care that people thought I was crazy, and sometimes my parents thought I was disrespectful because I didn't want the life they had. It's not disrespect, it's a different vision.

Of course, there were times that I didn't know exactly how to get where I was going, but I always knew the vision. If you make a wrong turn, correct it. The destination is still going to be there when you arrive. I also didn't broadcast my vision to everyone because it's only my business where I'm going, and small-minded people can't handle it. If you come from a background with a poor mentality, your big dreams aren't met with well-wishes. Poverty is certainly more than a mentality but gets embedded in the mind too. I was poor for years, but mentally knew I wouldn't remain that way. Even if something happens and I return to poverty, I know how to get back out. That's how good exposure, vision, drive and execution work.

What have you been working on that hasn't yet come into fruition? How could you enhance your execution?

____

____

____

____

____

____

____

____

____

____

Chapter 2: Shock & Shame - Living a Double Life

This chapter title stirs up weighted memories. Throughout my life, people knew me as determined, gregarious, and a top-performer, whether in class, my career, or on an athletic field. Because of my exposure, the literature I consume, and my rise (thank you, Maya Angelou), my trials and tribulations don't appear on my face. Listen, I don't look like where I come from. And I don't just mean my small town, but my household too. For example, my high school teachers thought the world of me and all of my friends. We were the top students, and many of us were also athletes, bringing home that Romulus Eagle pride.

As the eldest child, my teachers were ecstatic to hear that my younger siblings were going to be in their classes. You've already read about my siblings, but I didn't "warn" my teachers about my siblings' behavior or previous poor performance because anyone can change at any time. I let them go on believing that I was from a family that loved education and that my siblings would be their top students. I'm not going to slander people because they operate differently than I do. I'm also not going to lie to you and tell you that shock and shame weren't waiting for me behind many doors in life after people met my family. Part of the reason I didn't brief my teachers on my siblings was that I wasn't ready to face their shock or my shame.

This is the part that hurts. My parents told me to set a good example, and I did that as the eldest. There came a point when they stopped allowing me to post my high marks or awards in the house because it was seen as showing off. I'm glad my dad kept everything for me and I still have it. The example I was told to set, was seen as hurting others, instead of celebrated, so I didn't like attention. It made me uncomfortable. I thought being happy about my success was prideful and bragging. But it wasn't. It took me years to be able to accept attention again and to be able to sit comfortably in the warm light of my happiness.

Excelling was a huge deal for me, my friends and their families, but not for mine. My family thought I loved school, but actually, I loved leaving home. I loved getting into a circle where my insane thoughts of success were normal, expected and encouraged. When I showed up, I put my home life away and enjoyed myself. I felt like I was living a double life. With my friends, I lived. I laughed. I had wealth in my heart that couldn't be shaken.

When my teachers got my siblings as students after me, they were elated and expecting some version of the knowledge and respect they assumed I was bringing from home. In reality, I'd been studying other students and delving into written tales of people in faraway lands for years. When the dust settled after my siblings ran circles around them, threw textbooks away in class while storming out, broke hinges off of doors, or simply fell asleep from disinterest, those teachers immediately pulled me aside or met me after school, before practice. They always had the same questions.

Common Questions:

"How the hell did you end up like this, but your siblings like that?"

"What is going on at home?"

"Are you actually related to them?" or "Do you have the same parents?"

"Have your siblings always been like this?

"What do your parents do?"

The Answer:

Although we were all exposed to the same things initially, I spent my time differently, and stepped away and joined a different circle of friends. Those friends had parents who heralded knowledge and success. To them, I was another one of their children, and I appreciated the support.

At the time, I didn't have an answer. Mostly, I was ashamed. My teachers were intrigued because they knew there was more to the story. As an adult, I know that there is more beneath the surface, and I always have, but I was ashamed to be different. There were two sides to my shame. On one hand, I was ashamed that I couldn't fit in with my blood. Then I got to a point where I was so upset with people pointing out that I was different, that I wanted to hide my family all together. I didn't speak of them, or only briefly and vaguely. I then became ashamed of the parts of me that did fit in with them. Like my family, my patience was thin, and my temper was short. I liked lewd jokes, sparring, and messy gossip. I talked fast and couldn't sit still for long. I was struggling to tame the parts of me that were in the wind, so I could tie them neatly to the future vision I had of myself. Eventually, I was tamed beyond self-recognition and had to figure out who I was, and not just who I envisioned. It took stillness, patience, and time alone to think for myself. It took speaking up in situations that didn't feel right to my soul. I had to put my shame aside and embrace myself for who I am. Who I am, matters most on this journey, not where I'm from or where I want to go.

I was afraid to enter a relationship because I thought that if I took someone to meet my family, that person would quickly leave me for someone else with less baggage (or none). Meeting the right person helped me get past that.

I accepted where I came from as a part of me instead of as a fatal flaw that would ultimately bring me to my demise. People told me I was better than my family.

My family told me that I thought I was better than them, and maybe some people believed that I was from their insecurities. Being forced to face down differences as if they were inherently negative caused me shame. I had teachers and friends who expressed their shame at my upbringing and told me to get as far away from them as possible. I've also had people tell me to never make a mistake because it would kill my parents since my siblings were already so bad. Man! That's heavy to put on the shoulders of a teenager, and that's why I ended up in therapy in college.

Be mindful of what you say to people, especially kids. I don't care how mature you think they act. I was losing my mind because I thought I was supposed to be some familial savior. I thought I was supposed to go to college and then start a business that could pay for my entire family (extended included), to live their dream lives. That's not even my vision, but I felt like it was my duty in obedience. Whew! That's the stuff good therapy sessions are made of.

I want to produce great things for my legacy, but those are my children, grandchildren and beyond. It's also the people I can touch by being of service, whether older or younger. Part of being the rich sibling is having clarity.

Chapter 3: It's More Expensive to be Poor than Rich

Believe it or not, it's more expensive to be poor than it is to be rich. My investments pay for my luxuries, and in fact, many rich people can live for free. I live in the world of real estate and land use planning, so I see it every day. Here's how it works: landlords own properties, and their tenants pay for the cost of the building and the cost of the landlord to live for free. Your rent is usually higher than the cost of the mortgage for the property you stay in. That's because you're paying the mortgage, even if you don't own the building. Therefore, nearly everyone is involved in real estate. You're either an investor (landlord) or a tenant (renter). And sometimes you're a passive investor in real estate (e.g. Real Estate Investment Trust/REIT), without being a direct landlord, but for simplicity, we'll talk about direct ownership. Let's get some math behind it. We'll start small and scale-up.

Let's say you own a duplex. That's a multi-family home consisting of two attached units. Each unit has a separate entrance, which is why you may also hear this referred to as "two doors" when a landlord is counting units. Let's say the cost of the entire duplex property was $100,000. If you leverage the bank's money by taking out a loan, as many investors do, a 30-year mortgage at a 3% interest would make the total cost $151,778. Interest compounds over the 30 years, which makes the price higher than if you pay in full with cash. This breaks down to a mortgage payment of $421.60 per month for 30 years. Many of you are paying much more than that on your rent or mortgage. Meanwhile, your landlord is living for free! Think about it. As a renter, your job is paying for your landlord's housing too. Since the mortgage on the duplex is $421.60 per month, how much would you charge each unit for rent? In reality, you'd base that on the market rate. Some landlords hold the rent steady for a great tenant, or one that is struggling (you're the boss!). Let's say you charge double the mortgage payment for each unit. That's $843.20 rent per unit. You have the opportunity to bring in $1,686.40 total from the duplex each month. Or, you can live in one of the units, take the $843.20 per month from your other unit, and use it to pay the $421.60 for your building's mortgage, while keeping the other half. Since the mortgage is paid by your other tenant, you get to live for free! In fact, you're getting paid to live because you get to keep the remaining $421.60 since you charged double the mortgage for rent. That extra money can be used to pay down the mortgage faster, to invest in another property or asset, pay for maintenance fees, or to pay for whatever you assign the money to do. Make sure you have a plan for your money. At the same time you're getting paid to live, you're still building equity in the property and hopefully capitalizing on increasing property value as well.

If you decide to rent out both units, you can keep $1,264.80 after paying the mortgage. Of course, there are still costs for maintenance, and you may choose to use a property management company that takes a percentage of the monthly rent. The bottom line is, you can either pay someone $843 for rent, or you can make money to live rent-free.

30-Year Mortgage on Duplex: $151,778
Monthly Mortgage Payment: $421.60
Rent Price Tenants Pay: $843.20 per unit ($1,686.40 total for two)
Landlord's Rent Price: $0. Free!

The owner lives for free in one of the units and keeps the remaining $421.60 after paying the mortgage.

Let's scale up with a different scenario. The monthly mortgage on your 4-unit property is $1000. You charge each unit $2,000 per month for rent because it's an expensive area, but you were able to get a deal on a fixer-upper (a rundown property that you made look pretty again). Together the four units bring in $8,000 per month ($2,000 each). Subtract the rent, and you get to keep $7,000 every month. That's $84,000 per year. Even if you have another $1,000 in expenses each month, you'd still keep $6,000 per month or $72,000 per year. Don't forget to pay those taxes! As you move up, you can consider forming an LLC, transferring your property title to your LLC, and taking advantage of a lower tax rate. It's up to you. Imagine having 100 units across your portfolio, each paying $2,000 per month. That's $200,000 per month, and $2,400,000 per year, without factoring in the various possible expenses. That is what assets look like and why the rich get richer.

Meanwhile, the poor struggle to make ends meet. The poor struggle with rent payments, and the middle-class work to pay off their mortgages and other debts. When some people get extra cash or receive a lump sum of their own money via what's called a "tax refund" during tax season, they use it to buy liabilities. They buy things like new furniture or new carpet in a place they rent (not own), clothes, or make a down payment on a new car. Sure, vehicles can be used to make money via distribution centers or ride-sharing services, and one of my siblings does this, but the car note, and insurance combined, outweigh the money earned through those income sources. There is a benefit when a rare vehicle is sold for more than you paid for it, or when a vehicle helps you earn more than it's worth. Maybe you drive a $50,000 vehicle, but the vehicle attracts clients that pay you more than that per month, per project, or other transactions. This is how the rich think and behave. The poor use their hard-earned money to buy liabilities, while the rich use their assets to purchase more assets or the luxuries they desire. The rich do not owe payments on luxuries, which is why I don't refer to those luxuries as liabilities. If your assets pay you to travel the world, keep traveling the world. If your job or business covers your first class or private jet expenses, fly how you want! This is not to say that the poor can't or shouldn't have luxuries. Those luxuries shouldn't jeopardize your ability to pay for your cost of living, or they are liabilities.

Some "experts" will recommend that you have three to six months of expenses saved in an emergency fund. I disagree. What happens when the emergency outlasts your savings? What happens when you exhaust those funds, and new emergency hits a month later? Poverty feels like one emergency after another. First your car goes down, then your electricity bill is higher than it usually is, you've put more than you can afford on credit cards, now you're facing a rent increase as you renew the lease, and your child is sick. I used to neglect my vehicle because I couldn't afford basic maintenance. One day the engine died at the gas station and I had to walk home along a busy road. I couldn't pay for a taxi or ride-share service. I didn't know how I'd get to work the next day. Luckily a colleague was willing to pick me up before work. You can't save for an emergency, while constantly living in an emergency or crisis.

You need to have investments working for you at all times, so that nothing financial truly feels like an emergency. The first step is to figure out how much you cost. How much does it cost to run your entire life and your household every month? Multiply that by 12 to determine how much you cost every year. If you have a family (children, spouse, parent(s) living with you), include those expenses. That cost may be higher than what you earn, which is why you're in debt. This total should include how much you'd like to save and invest. Once you get your total, you know how much you need to earn from your investments. To practice for your future, research the cost of all of the things you want to have and how much you'd ideally save and invest. That's the next level of what your investments need to earn for you. Maybe your dream costs $100,000 per year. Maybe it costs $100,000 per month, or $1,000,000 per month.

What's Your Number?

How much does it currently cost to be you? Housing, vehicle, meals, personal development, travel, family expenses etc.

Expenses	Monthly Cost	Annual Cost
__Total:__		

How Much Does the Vision Cost?

Do your research. How much will it cost to live in your vision? Travel, spas, residences, fine dining, entertainment, personal development, professional development etc.

Vision Expenses	Monthly Cost	Annual Cost
Vision Total:		

Keep your number in mind when considering investments. You can't hit your target if you don't know what to look for. If your investments have you covered, you can use your job's income as money to give, start another business, or put in trusts for your children and grandchildren. If you don't like your job or what you do, you can do something you love instead. If you love what you do, you're already winning! Prepare for life, not an emergency.

Everyone should invest in themselves and position themselves in a place where they can live financially free, and most importantly, with financial confidence and time. Time is the most important asset, not money, so figure out how to maximize your time, by using money as the tool it is. That's all money is—a tool. You can't build a house without tools. You can't prepare a good meal for your family without tools. Money is a tool that too many people don't have in their toolbox when it's time to build a better life. When economic downturns and pandemics strike the world, they hit the poor the hardest. The rich don't panic because they have the tools to keep building. Financial confidence is the knowledge of how to use money as a tool, combined with the fortitude to face and overcome monetary obstacles. Even if you don't have the money, financial confidence means you know where to find that tool again and how to use it efficiently when you get it.

Some people think they have financial confidence because they don't care about how they spend money. They spend with excitement and enthusiasm because you can't take any money with you when you die. I was raised with the phrase, "You can't take it with you." The idea that earning money is chasing after the wind because you can't do anything with it when you die. Ha! It's not about what you can take with you, it's about what you can leave behind. Life is about legacy and legacy is so much more than money. However, would you rather saddle your descendants or successors with debt, or set them up to continue to bear fruit. When I hear the term "heir" or "heiress", I think of someone who stands to inherit a legacy. Most families don't use those terms because nobody's getting shit! I wasn't raised hearing my parents talk to my siblings and me as their heirs. However, my spouse and his siblings were in constant dialogue with their family about their role as ambassadors for their royal family name. I married into the Ikharo Royal Family, of Auchi, Nigeria (Edo State), and I love seeing how our Nigerian family works continuously to extend the legacy. To know that your grandfather, or father, was king (called "Otaru" in the Auchi language) and that you or one of your descendants could hold the throne is an honor. Sure, the children are lectured hard about the importance of legacy, which can be off-putting to most legacy children, but their generation can change and enhance that conversation for descendants to come.

I've been able to witness people across the Ikharo Royal Family contribute to various accounts that support different causes or family functions. I didn't know that some families had routine (monthly or quarterly) conference calls to address the state of the family, contributions and future spending. It opened my eyes to how an entire family (extended included) can function as a unit. This doesn't mean there aren't disagreements (sometimes harsh), but it's a glimpse into what's possible for my legacy. That bond keeps a family wealthy.

Chapter 4: How to Buy Happiness

You've probably heard the phrase: "Money can't buy happiness." Whoever says this, doesn't know where to shop. Here's what I mean. Money affords the opportunity to buy joyful experiences, donate more to causes you believe in, and provides freedom from survival-based financial worries, like affording day to day expenses. The added stress of crowdfunding for money to pay for a funeral when a loved one dies, or medical expenses after a sudden illness, can be eliminated. Being able to buy exactly what you want, when you want it, will make you happy for a while. Not just cars, handbags, and yachts, but exotic travel at the drop of a hat, culinary experiences at *home* with renowned chefs. You can have your favorite masseuse who knows all of your tension spots and comes to meet you wherever you are in the world, the best trainers and doctors for your fitness and health needs, and a 24/7 concierge.

The next level of happiness is to bring the people you love along for this journey. One of the best things about money is the ability to be increasingly generous. Seeing other people happy and making a real difference in their lives, makes me deeply happy. It's one thing to be able to donate $100 for a student to buy books, but it's another to be able to give $100,000 so that a student can graduate debt-free or start that business they've been planning. There are stories of people donating millions so that an entire graduating class is debt-free. Generosity is rewarding. I used to want to win the lottery, now I want to be a lottery for others. That doesn't mean I'm shelling out money, time, or other resources to everyone or even half of the people who ask. Loving to give and knowing kindness doesn't equate to naivete. Generosity shouldn't always involve money and should never involve you being taken advantage of. Be vigilant!

One of the happiest moments of my life was when I was able to surprise my aunt, who helped raise me, with a first-class trip to her dream destination. She cried and told me that it was the first time in her life, that she was going to be able to have real fun. As one of her parents' eldest daughters, she had to raise her younger eight siblings and cook for the family. From there, she went on to work and have children of her own. Since I grew up hearing her tell these stories of early responsibility and dreams of getting away, I vowed in my heart to send her on her dream vacation when I got older. I never told her about it, but I had the vision of taking her. The crazy thing is, she'd already purchased clothing for that trip years in advance and hung them in her closet. Because of her faith, she knew one day she'd make it to her tropical paradise.

Where is that place in the world that you'd like to go to, or someone you love would like to go? Find out.

My mom loves Barcelona, Spain. The first time I took her, I used the extra scholarship money I had from school. My part-time internship wasn't paying much, but I knew my mom was stressed out and needed a vacation. She had a passport that was expiring soon, but she'd never used it. Since Spring Break was coming up, I bought us a trip to Barcelona, with the help of my sister who paid for half of our mom's plane ticket. Though we didn't have much money to spend, we had the trip of a lifetime. One night, we walked along the port to look at the cruise ships. After a while, we got chilly by the water and needed to use the restroom. We saw a huge hotel in the distance, so we ventured towards it in the crisp night. When we walked in, the floors in the lobby sparkled like stars, and our eyes danced up the spiral staircase. It was the World Trade Center of Barcelona, which happens to have a wonderful hotel.

Seeing the awe in my mother's eyes, I said, "Next time we come to Barcelona, we're going to stay here. Beside the marina." I don't know if she believed me, but we were back three years later, with plenty to spend on an unplanned Thanksgiving weekend getaway in Barcelona. A couple of weeks before the trip, I called her up to see if she had Thanksgiving plans. She thought I was talking about going the following year since Thanksgiving was only a couple of weeks away. I said, "We're going in two weeks and we can stay at that 5-star hotel we saw last time on the marina." She was excited! My mom and I had great experiences whether we had money or not. However, the freedom we had on that second trip was a million times more fun. We spent half as much time in Barcelona on our second trip, but we were able to do more because we had the funds to capitalize on our time. The vistas were better, the service was exquisite, and we could hop in a cab to go long distances quickly, instead of riding the train, which we also did when time allowed. We rented electric scooters and powered through the city we love. We even chatted in Spanish with local shop owners we'd remembered from before. Travel and family mean everything in my life, so these experiences mean the world to me. More than the world. If being the rich sibling allows me to pave a way for my mom and my descendants, it's what I'll choose every time. As for my siblings, I help guide them when they ask me because I believe in teaching an able person to fish rather than subsidizing their lives. In teaching others to fish, we cannot make them start fishing.

Discover what makes you happy and do it. Don't buy things to impress people, or to fit in, because those things will eat at your soul, instead of strengthening you. Happiness isn't an object; it's a state of being. That's why people say, "Money can't buy happiness." But, you can buy things that help place you in that happy state of being. If you want to take your children on a magical getaway, do it! Surprise them with the time of their lives. "Wake up, kids! We're going to Disney World today!" Or to Nairobi, Kenya on an amazing safari, and to see an elephant orphanage. Whatever it is that interests their young hearts. Watch them light up! If your children are adults now, you can still have great trips with them. Or do something else for someone you love. My spouse and I went to Disney World together because we never went as children. We got to be kids again! There is so much in the world to do and see. But once again, that's what excites me and the people I love. Figure out what excites your people and do it!

What excites you and the people you love?

____

____

____

____

____

____

____

____

____

____

____

____

____

____

____

Chapter 5: Blue-Collar Flashbacks - Rich but Operating in Poverty

A "Blue-Collar Flashback" is when you have abundance, but you accidentally make a decision as if you're still in poverty. A poverty mentality is when all of your decisions come from a place of lack. One of the hardest things to overcome is a poverty mentality. It took me a while to realize that wealthy people, with healthy, well-rounded lives, didn't just have different amounts of money. They had different minds. I thought I only wanted my vision and all the good and peace I was exposed to, but what I wanted was a mindset shift. When you're accustomed to living in lack, and fear of creating more debt, you learn how to stretch a dollar. That's an important skill to have, but it can be debilitating.

If you fly first class to a destination and then automatically try to take a bus to your hotel instead of paying for a taxi, that's a "Blue Collar Flashback". Many hotels and first-class tickets include shuttles or private drivers, so hearing a steep taxi price to your distant hotel may induce a flashback if you're not used to seeing it anymore. It's a good thing to have sometimes because it reminds us of how far we've come. If you're flying private, a driver should already be there for you when you land. Always consider what your time is worth. If the express metro is a faster option, go for it. If you need space to work privately, to relax, or for security, pay for a driver. The same goes for getting around in any city you're traveling to. I love having a local, professional driver who knows where to go, and all of the best spots, giving me a tour. Don't let a Blue-Collar Flashback make you spend hours getting lost on a hot bus, crowded metro, or on the back of someone's motorbike down rocky roads. Sure, you could meet new people while lost and have fun, but if you already have plans, that's not the way to start. Get lost when you have time and patience for a mishap. That's why time is a beloved asset.

One of my Blue-Collar Flashbacks happened during a day trip from San Francisco to Los Angeles, California. I flew my mom and me down to LA to shop, eat and go to the beach. That is in essence a luxury day trip. When we landed in LA, we waited nearly an hour for the Hollywood shuttle to take us to Hollywood, because it's what I once did as a student, instead of getting a taxi immediately. What were we waiting on? At some point my mom turned to me and asked, "Why didn't we just get a taxi, to begin with?" It was a Blue-Collar Flashback. We wanted that hour back but couldn't get it! Time is the most valuable thing in the world. Money, you can make, the time you cannot. We still had an amazing day trip gallivanting around LA before hailing a taxi back to the airport, and off to chilly San Francisco.

I'll make a point of distinction between Blue-Collar

Flashbacks and being frugal. Frugality isn't optional in poverty. It's just life. Being frugal is an action that people who are at least middle class take to save money. It's a financial choice. Poverty is reactive, not proactive like frugality. However, a Blue-Collar Flashback is when you forget you have options because you were impoverished for so long. I'm grateful and blessed to be able to momentarily forget that I have options and to remember again.

What were some of your Blue-Collar Flashbacks?

____

____

____

____

____

____

____

____

____

____

____

____

Chapter 6: Stealth Wealth

Stealth wealth is when you have money but don't flaunt it. Blue Collar Flashbacks come in handy when concealing your net worth because money is still a taboo subject in many settings. Vigilance is often necessary, especially when traveling. This isn't about living in fear, it's about being smart. I've had my money and my phone stolen by people I knew, and we were all poor or middle class. I was at what was supposed to be an intimate party, and voila, my shit was gone. I no longer hang out with them, but they taught me a valuable lesson. When people see a sucker, they lick it. Don't operate as a target around shooters. Theft happens at all income levels, so playing it cool is always in favor. My sister bought a new car and it was stolen immediately while visiting a friend's house. Even if you have security present, stealth matters. Not sure who came up with this gem, but, "True power hides in plain sight." There's something to be said about those who look like they're hanging out with friends but are with their bodyguards.

It's often easy to spot someone who isn't rich because they wear clothing with brand logos plastered all over themselves. The same people who shell out cash for fashion (real or knockoffs), may not have enough food in the pantry to feed themselves or their children. There are people who cover themselves in designer logos who are rich, but I tend to see it more among the poor and middle-class. Quality is evident without designer stamps across your chest. I've known people who'd leave the price tags on so others could see it! It was a consumption show for others. I don't usually wear obvious designer labels because I don't want to look like I work for your company. If you're not endorsing me, or sponsoring a collaborative event, I'm not actively advertising your brand. That's free advertising for you, and usually a loss for me. However, there are occasions and professions where tailored suits and stunning gowns attract more clients, press, fans, and opportunities to bill at higher rates. Other than a gala, ceremony, or special business opportunity, you probably won't know which brand I'm wearing, or where I got my clothes. Most of my wardrobe is bespoke in Nigeria. In my day to day life, or football season, you'll catch me in a University of Michigan (Go Blue!) or University of Virginia (Wahoowa!) shirt because those are my alma maters, and I paid for them.

We live in a society of consumers, and a few producers. That's one of the key causes of our continued wealth gap. The producers get richer and the consumers get poorer. As the rich sibling, I'm constantly searching for new things to learn, produce or get involved in. My goal as a producer is to make sure I'm helping people. There are so many useless products in the world, but they still sell because consumers live to buy. My existence was never centered on profiting solely for myself; it's about creating opportunities for my descendants and making those before me proud because their fight bore fruit. I want to help people, especially those who struggled like me, or far more than I ever did.

Consumers don't practice stealth wealth because they live to show off what they've bought. Technology allows consumers to compare their lives to other consumers outside of their tax bracket. Producers love it! The producers who prey on envy, rule capitalism. You may think they're posting pictures of their private jets, and private islands to inspire you, but ultimately, it's for you to invest in them instead of yourself. Consumers think that buying into a brand through products, makes them part of the brand. However, unless you're a shareholder or the owner, you don't hold a stake in that company. Stop trying to impress the people around you and impress the person inside of you instead.

When my father passed, my siblings and I all received trust accounts containing $12,000. To withdraw from the account, we had to withdraw a minimum of $250 at a time. I was 20, my sister was 18, and our brother was 17; he had to wait a year before he could access the money because he was a minor. As teenagers and a 20-year-old me, we thought we had it made. The lottery winning mentality in full swing. That was 2010, and a great time to purchase real estate following the Great Recession in the U.S. Money was cheap because rates were low. That means you could borrow money from banks at lower interest rates and pay a smaller amount in total over time.

Did any of us buy real estate or other investments with our trusts? No! Did our mom suggest any financial routes we could take? No! She didn't know any. I don't know what my siblings bought, but I paid rent, traveled to nearby cities, and bought $300 watches, and designer handbags until it was all gone. I don't have any of those items today, which means I have nothing to show for $12,000. On the other hand, Timothy Sykes, an investor, turned the $12,000 from his Bar Mitzvah into $2,000,000 before he was 30. The difference in mindset between the rich and poor is insane! I wasn't even making $12,000 per year at my job, but I spent a $12,000 account on liabilities within a year. Afterward, I spent years kicking myself for flushing $12,000, before I was able to get over it. I decided to simply earn it back and do better.

When I first got my hands on that $12,000 trust in college, stealth wealth was the furthest thing from my mind. I couldn't wait to look rich at my fancy university, full of real rich kids. That was foolish, but eventually, I learned. I'd say I grew up, but aging, unfortunately, doesn't equate to financial literacy. Had I invested it, I'd have something to show for it today— a portfolio. That's because stealth wealth thinks long-term, instead of short-term. Playing rich for a few months to a year is nothing like living the rest of your life in financial freedom.

How much money have you wasted over the years?

I grew up hearing about men who'd drive beater cars to the businesses they owned in high-crime areas, but have a Bentley parked at home. That's stealth wealth. I found myself practicing stealth wealth without thinking about it. I own a nice vehicle, but I usually take the train because it's faster than sitting in traffic. A friend's father lives in the Middle East and has a dedicated driver because he sits in traffic for several hours a day traveling between business meetings. He opted for a luxury vehicle because it's a mobile living room for him as he works from the road. I didn't buy my car to impress thieves or to ride to work. I bought it because I enjoyed it on my test drive, and it's equally comfortable as a passenger. Still, I take the train because it's practical. If I'm too dressed up to bother with being harassed on the Metro, I take a taxi.

However, I had no idea that ride-hailing services presented a major class issue. In Michigan, people drive as the norm, so I wasn't familiar with the ins and outs of well-off people taking cabs when I moved to the Washington, DC area. I found myself in a situation where I told an associate (friend of a friend) that I was taking a cab home, and she exclaimed, "Oh! I can tell you're rich." The cab was only going to cost $10, but she didn't know that. She only knew that I was paying money for a taxi instead of taking the train or driving like everyone else. At first, I tried to play it cool like I used to do, to fit in, but then I gave up on trying to code-switch in the middle of the night and took my ass home...in a taxi. Sometimes rich people slip up and say privileged things in the wrong environment. I recognize that and own it. I don't like being insensitive or inconsiderate. However, I'm not going to rough it in the middle of the night to prove I haven't "changed" or progressed. I have and that's ok. Being myself could expose someone to new opportunities and change his life, like my classmates did for me. I don't have time for hoop-jumping and people-pleasing, so sometimes, you may hear something that strikes you as spoiled, but I broke my back for everything I have, so I truly don't care if I spoil myself now.

I cared for so long about what people thought of me, that I lost myself. I don't intentionally say things to hurt people because I believe my purpose in life is to make a difference through service. Being happily rich shouldn't hurt other people, but it reminds them of inequalities. No one should be excluded from opportunities. Barring exclusionary practices, people who don't do what you do, shouldn't get what you get. Here's the other thing, legacy. We can't all start from the same place if someone's mother or fifth-great-grandfather started this wealth process generations ago. I made this book about siblings, at the core, to show how divides can begin even with level playing fields.

People are intentionally hiding wealth from others to prevent uncomfortable conversations. I'm not just talking about the wealth gap conversation, but also some people you know constantly asking for money. Situations like your cousin, whom you barely know, asking you to invest in his business without having a business plan or a track record of execution. Today no one knows your uncle is rich because he loaned his brother money once and never heard from him again. He started practicing stealth wealth, even around his extended family. If you're the rich sibling, parent, aunt/uncle, or cousin, you'll find that few family members will ask how you built wealth, and if you can guide them, or point them in the right direction. I'd rather hear that! They want instant gratification. Wealth isn't instant! Conversations are generally surface level (e.g. how's the weather? how's work?). Sometimes this is just to make it look like they don't always ask for money when they contact you, but eventually the ask appears. It may start off as, "Can you do me a favor?" Or, come at the end of a dramatic story.

And what about your poor siblings?

I truly care that my siblings are poor. I do want to help with financial literacy and have done so. It doesn't mean that I'm passing out money or other resources to them because I don't believe in enabling bad financial habits. Also, they're not my children. To be honest, I wouldn't frivolously pass out money to my children either. I believe in earning your keep. As Warren Buffett said, "You should leave your children enough so they can do anything, but not enough so they can do nothing." It's hard for many people to become financially free because they are tied to obligations with their extended family: adult siblings, cousins, aunts, uncles and beyond. It is honorable to help your family and friends when you can and when you want. However, if your kids can't have opportunities because you're paying extended family members, something needs to change.

Several of my father's friends only came around when he had money. They weren't really his friends at all. His real friends were few and were hard on him because they wanted him to get it together. Yet every payday, I'd see the same faces at our house. They were smiling and talking loudly. Money brought excitement. His friends knew that he was generous and would pay for everything, including what's considered to be top-shelf drugs and alcohol. They are alive, he is not. While it's great to be generous, your friends and family members shouldn't be using you, and only seeing you on payday, or asking you for money.

Chapter 7: How to Loan Money to Family

To get to wealth, you have to stop carrying dead weight. People who say they love you will hop on your finances with all of their sob stories and ride you to the ground. They'll ride you through the ground if you let them! They'll quote scriptures of why you should give to them, though they don't give to anyone. Some of them will preface an ask with "I hate asking for money," but then ask you anyway. I don't know about you, but I don't usually do things I hate. You cannot build wealth as a bad steward of what you already have in life.

Unless you have a Family Bank set up with trustees and legal paperwork, or want to give something freely, just say, "No!" when your extended family members ask for money. You should know when the relationship you have with a person isn't authentic. Blood alone won't make people love you. As a good person you should give of yourself, and the best people are good even to those who persecute them but don't be foolish in when, how, or to whom you choose to give. Don't pay people who don't care about you as a sign of blood loyalty or because they're old friends. They're extended family and old friends for a reason. Your extended family consists of anyone outside of your chosen, adult household. This is not the household you grew up in. If you live alone, you are the sole nucleus of your family. If you are married, your immediate family is you, your spouse, and any children you have. Your siblings become extended family when you're grown because you'll all start to form your own families. You can categorize "extended" and "immediate" however you want to, but it's an immediate "No" from me unless I decide to buy you what you need, instead of giving cash.

I love giving and I do it cheerfully, but extortion is unacceptable. "Give me money because you have it, and I don't know how to save it." That's foolish. "Give me money because I have an unbelievable business idea that's going to make me rich." If you believe in it, work for it! I've known of clients giving away millions to family and friends because they all said they had great business ideas. I don't invest in things I don't know. I dislike when people forgo building real relationships or offering services before asking for money. I also dislike people asking for discounts on services because we're the same gender or ethnicity. Feel free to support me because we look alike, but don't use it to try to take advantage of my business and kindness.

Let's get deeper. There are a couple of common ways to deal with family and money. One is gifting, and the other is loaning. If you give money to family, make sure you know it's a gift. That means, no one is automatically expected to pay you back or owe you in any way. You need to know that it's a gift, or you will harbor feelings of resentment the first time that person disrespects or disregards you after your loving donation. Money aside, no one should be disrespecting you, but after you've paid that person, the disrespect has more bite to it. If you're giving, to later receive, that's not a true gift--it's a loan. You need to first be clear with yourself. If you want to loan money, get it in writing. Not everyone is going to establish a Family Bank, but it is a long-term wealth option. Their word and a handshake won't cut it when it comes to a loan, especially with family.

Family plays to your heart and sensitivities, and so does money. For that reason, family and money can create conflict down to our heartstrings. Our hearts are attached to the things we treasure, and we may lie to ourselves about the order of importance of those things. However, your heart knows the truth. You may say you treasure your cousin or brother more than $50,000, or a million dollars, but when he can't repay the loan, the knives come out. Get a contract on the terms of the loan, including when payments will be due and how much they'll be. What are the consequences of default? It's called a high-risk loan for a reason. Make sure both parties understand the terms, sign documents saying they understand the terms and get it all notarized. Then file it virtually and get hard copies. Cover your bases! Your family members or friends may say that you don't trust them, but it's your money that they asked for. It's not about trust, it's about responsibility and boundaries. You have a responsibility to yourself and to your time. It takes time to chase your sister around for money you lent her to get her car fixed, even though she wears a new outfit every day, goes on luxury vacations and buys new furniture every few months. I often ask my siblings and others how they'd get the money if I don't lend it, and what the outcome would be if they don't get it from anywhere. Their projected outcomes won't change my decision, but I hope it helps them look at alternatives.

Chapter 8: Time & Boundaries

"Time & Boundaries" can easily be two separate chapters or separate books, but I grouped them because setting boundaries will save you time. Saying "No" doesn't make you a bad person--it means you care about your time. One of the biggest boundaries that rich siblings (and rich parents) have to set, is a financial boundary. The next is time. The requestor may not want to spend time with you at all, but what they're asking you to do takes time. I can sense when someone wants to ask me for something. As a rich sibling, it's hard to see people you love struggle to make ends meet, but I also see them make poor decisions. Saying "No" doesn't mean you can't be generous. However, not all giving is healthy for them or you. When I know someone burns through money, I don't feel inclined to give them money. However, I am always open to talk to them about how to invest, budget and live within their means. My goal is to be an example of financial freedom so that others can claim their freedom. My goal is not to enable able-bodied adults to sleep in my wallet.

Furthermore, when it comes to my time, I am not anyone's personal assistant. My brother asked me if I was a secretary because it was his only guess of what I could be doing. I love secretaries and assistants, but it's not my calling. I will ruin your schedule. Being of service to others doesn't mean I'm going to research your business idea and write the plan. I also do not have time to help you edit a grant for a bid or a non-profit. Hire a professional or a volunteer with that skill set if you don't have the funds. There are great projects that I don't have time to take on. Sometimes I'll brainstorm with you if I have a background in your interest. However, I will not waste my time if I don't have it to give. Loaning time is more precious than loaning money, but we don't have family banks or institutional banks for that. People will want to "pick your brain" and spend countless hours with you, but you need to set boundaries. You can't pay my spouse to do something if he doesn't want to do it. There is no price because his time is invaluable. I learned the true meaning of invaluable from him. He's a brilliant linguist, in multiple languages, and I offered to pay him all types of money to do some editing for me, but he would not. I tried to barter with him using other things, but he would not budge. I had fun trying, and I know he loves me, but he didn't have time because it wasn't his preferred editing content. He prefers fiction, not non-fiction. I respect his boundaries because I love him and because I respect myself.

I don't know how much time people have asked me for, but I'm frugal with it. You should be too! I've had loads of stress in my life, so the free time I have is for me, and the people I choose. To some people, I may seem brief, yet friendly. It's because time is valuable, but not enough to be a complete asshole. I don't say or engage too much with certain people because they will attempt to get a full, unpaid therapy session out of me. Hire a professional. We can talk, and I can lend an ear from time to time, but I will not be used as a therapist or a decision-maker in your life. My advice consists of me asking you a couple of questions and stepping aside for you to decide for yourself. There are times when my siblings want me to babysit my nieces and nephews. I love them, but I don't always have time to be a caretaker. When I do have time, I pull out all the stops. We have a blast. At other times, I help them with homework virtually. Having long-term wealth in time and money requires boundaries.

I've had grown men in my family ask me to loan them thousands of dollars. They didn't even blink. They either offered me my money back at some unknown time in the future or with a little interest on top. Give me a break! Whenever you get a loan from the bank, that bank wants you to pay them monthly! And if you're late on a payment, you have to pay interest and sometimes additional penalties. That's usury, but it's life. Listen, if you can't pay a bank back (even without interest), you won't be able to pay me back without interest, so I'm not interested. People, especially family, will ask you to pay upfront for their whole business because you're related. If I pay for you to start your business, that's now my business. That's how stock in a company works, and how a Family Bank is set up. If you don't pay your mortgage, or car note, it belongs to the bank. If I gift you the money to start your business because you came to me with a strong plan, with financial projections (or a Pro-forma), and I believe in you, that's one thing, but a loan is another matter entirely. If I don't know you to have a track record of responsibility, you're not getting a loan from me. That's a boundary I have to set. Most of the time, you don't need to show me a business plan because I've already seen your actions. I don't need to see the shit you've smeared on a hundred pages. Save a tree and have a seat instead.

I am equally vigilant about my time. How are you going to make my time with you worth it, especially if I don't value my time spent with you as equal? That's where generosity comes in, but you must have boundaries. Know how much time you're willing to give, when and to whom. What can that person do with their time, to add value to you?
Often, there are other ways for them to get what they need, but it's up to you to decide when to give. If someone is truly in need, and I feel led to give to that person, I will either give money, time or buy what it is they need. Usually, I buy what it is they need, as a personal preference. Giving doesn't have to be money, though it often is. I do not expect anything in return, but I would love for them to pay it forward if they see someone else in need in the future, or to the generations coming behind them.

To save time, I usually recommend the people I know to seek credit unions or banks, but often they don't want to go to banks because the banks have already said, No, because of their poor credit or poor history with that bank. If you already owe the bank $1,000 from overdrafts, or you are in default for $5,000, they won't want to lend you more. It's a high risk. Those aren't large sums of money for banks or credit unions, but it's a sign that you haven't been responsible with money, even in smaller amounts. If you can't steward over a little, you can't steward over a lot. Just like if you'd lie about a little, you'd lie about a lot. There are people who want to be millionaires, but don't have bank accounts. That doesn't make financial sense.

Good stewards of money and other goods tend to receive more, while poor stewards lose more. This is also written as the "Parable of Talents" or "Parable of Minas/Pounds". The person who was able to steward more was given more and produced more with it. It's good to be fruitful! I'm not talking about the people who are unbanked and don't trust banks because those particular banks have done shitty, unjust things to their communities. Many of them are now making life work just fine with credit unions, or some other financial system that feels supportive. I'm talking about the people who constantly have their hand out at someone else's table, but never have anything to bring. They offer promises but no guarantee. "If you lend me money, I promise to pay you back." I can't feed my household on a promise. I can't help uplift communities with promises. My soul loves hope, but my body starves on hope alone. I have to put in work. My money works. My faith works. I'm surrounded by work. I love people who execute on their goals because they put in work.

Many people I know of in my family don't have bank accounts. The reasons are varied, as discussed above. I *must* have *boundaries* because if loaning money, we're talking about entering an agreement with a person that doesn't involve a financial account. This is about loaning, not giving, which is different because it's a gift and doesn't have to be paid back. I know someone who had over a million dollars in bonds stored in a box in the attic, but that person also had financial accounts with at least as much. You can have a safe or vault in a private location of your choosing, but if you're aiming for financial freedom, you should also have some sort of financial account to interact with the growing wealth of the world. I don't feel comfortable lending money to someone without a financial account and a fiduciary relationship. Sharing a blood relationship doesn't make it comfortable.

Choosing to cash your checks at a check-cashing establishment, which keeps a percentage of your check as a service fee, is not a wise financial decision. It's a decision I've seen too much! Those without financial accounts often use check cashing places if they can't get a check cashed at work or a financial institution. Therefore, if I write a check, and you go to a check-cashing establishment, 10% of my loan to you goes to someone else. Those establishments generally keep between 1% and 12%

of each check they cash. I will not loan money, goods, or other resources to poor stewards. I'm not concerned with the great business ideas of poor stewards, and I wouldn't recommend it. Always set boundaries to protect your time and other resources.

Chapter 9: Wealthy Relationships - Inducting an Inner Circle

This is one of my favorite chapters. The most important thing I have in my life is my inner circle. In high school, I originally referred to my closest friends as the "Inner Party" because I loved George Orwell's novel, Nineteen Eighty-Four. The novel contains very realistic class divisions, but for us, the "Inner Party" was simply a clever name for a special group of friends. This is the life of nerds, and I love it. The people you choose to keep close to you, will shape your life. When kingdoms fall, it often starts from the inside. That means, someone inside the kingdom helped someone else on the outside bring it down. However, a strong inner circle can conquer and withstand all. If the people in your circle can't help you heal, grow and excel, you're in the wrong circle. If you're the smartest or wisest person in the group, you're in the wrong circle. Many of us know what it's like to be the leader of a group. However, a circle has no head or tail. Everyone in your inner circle needs to add wealth and positive energy. There are times when we all face obstacles, but if your life is always submerged in negativity, check your inner circle. You may be surrounded by bloodsuckers, or you may be the problem.

Discernment is key. I use the word "induct" because

choosing members shouldn't be taken lightly. In the past, I surrounded myself with people who lived near me. It had little to do with character, morals, or vision, just proximity. We lived in the same area or went to the same schools, and maybe we liked the same songs, played the same sports, or disliked the same things. In some instances, our parents grew up together. As we stayed together over the years, I got comfortable because of the time we'd spent. Our conversations centered on nostalgia, and nothing about our futures together was discussed. If the conversations were about the present, we each had enough familial drama to fill the room. However, as I executed on aspects of my vision, or shared details with them, I could feel the tension between us. I was rising to a new standard, alone. Sometimes the people in your circle will grow with you, but it's a rare gem. When I moved away, I got to know myself, and new people. I realized I'd been in a group that hated making new friends and was proud of it. To them, it was a sign of loyalty. It had nothing to do with character and shutting the door on poor morals.

That loyalty was trapping us in a box that wasn't transforming. We knew one another for who we were formerly, and not who we presently were, or who we were becoming. It was easy to speak briefly about a few things we wanted in life, but no one around me was executing. It was all talk. I grew up around all talk and no action and had chosen to align myself with people like I'd always known. It was familiar. It was comfortable. Realizing I was stagnant was a rude awakening. If you want something different, you have to let go of the familiar. You don't have to kick everyone to the curb if you don't want to, but you need to reorganize your life and your inner circle. That includes family.

My inner circle originally consisted of my family: parents, siblings, cousins, and grandparents. Some of my most counterproductive advice came from that circle. This is not disrespect, but the facts of my life. Listen, if you don't want someone's lifestyle, don't take that person's advice. Be respectful of their suggestions, but don't take them to heart. I began switching gears in middle school and aligned myself with peers who were talking about goals, and having fun. I was being pushed to grow up too fast because I was seen as "mature beyond my years," but I wanted to be a kid. I avoided the 12 and 13-year-olds who were having sex, doing drugs and getting pregnant. That wasn't fun for me. Since I never had a sex talk with my parents, I had to make sexual decisions on my own. The most important decision I made as a kid was to stop relying on my family to guide me. That may sound harsh, but whenever I listened to them, I got deeper into trouble. Most of us are taught blind obedience to authority as kids, but I had to wake up. I felt trapped in a life that wasn't meant for me. When I see children or older students battling with depression and thoughts of suicide because of their home life, I feel for them. I feel for you. Being 12 or 13 years old is truly a coming of age.

It was at 13 that I decided which university I wanted to go to, during a math field trip to the school. My family encouraged me to look towards community college instead, but I wanted to go to the University of Michigan. I decided to lean on my teachers, and friends' parents for encouragement and guidance. I thank God for the opportunity to be in the room with people who could truly see me, and genuinely wanted the best for me. That is what an inner circle should look like. It should feel warm and like a spiritual home. When you leave a reunion with them, or after a phone call, you should feel rejuvenated. You should feel loved. You shouldn't feel drained. I'm so glad I learned how to love, encourage and respect people. I aspired to be like the people I read about, such as Oprah Winfrey, Warren Buffett, Robert Kiyosaki and later, Dr. Eric Thomas and Jemal King. Their life stories, though different, resonated with me.

My siblings and I were, and are still, part of different circles. Since many important formative conversations weren't happening at home, we each learned about life in our separate groups, especially with our agemates. Because I was a few years older, we went to different schools after I left elementary school. By the time I was in high school, my sister was in middle school, and my brother was still in primary school. I didn't know many of their friends, but I knew a few. My brother was a gamer, so he hung out with gamers.

My sister was drawn to excitement and gossip, so she hung with kids who were infamous in school and around the neighborhood. We were all so different, that our peers didn't know that any of us were related. It doesn't matter if you share the same parents-- people are different. Those differences are more pronounced as inner circles change, education changes, finances change, spirituality changes, and anything else you can name.

I've heard many birth order stories that say that because I'm the eldest, I am driven to lead and be successful. That logic would make every eldest a leader. People are just different. I'm a successful eldest child, yet I married a successful middle child. I'm friends with the successful youngest of families. Some parents have all successful, happy adult children. When I talk about success, remember that I'm talking about freedom and options. In becoming successful, nature matters a ton, but it's the nurture of our peers, not just parents, that shape us most. Your inner circle matters so much. I could tell you that you're the average of the five people you spend the most time with, or I can tell you that you're just like your best friend(s). If you're happy with where you are, that's outstanding! However, if you're unhappy, look internally, and look at the people around you.

Who's in Your Inner Circle?

This probably isn't enough space to write about the people you hold dear but think about the people you're surrounded by. Would they include you in their circle as well?

Name	Why You Love This Person

Chapter 10: Maintaining a Wealthy Marriage

I'd be remiss if I didn't take the time to highlight the best part of my inner circle: my spouse. There is no way that my joys would be as high as they are without my spouse. My lows would be much lower without love. Yes, I was happy and content with my life while I was single. However, my spouse elevated me internally to a place I couldn't reach alone. Our marriage is a wealth of its own. It's rich in love, support, encouragement, kindness, romance, tenderness and joy.

Before we were married, we received counseling to prepare us for our lifelong journey together. This counseling came from a professional who also had a wealthy marriage. Use discernment in choosing who's allowed to counsel any of your relationships, especially your marriage. This person should be a professional and have what it is you're working towards. It's just like financial advice. I don't seek financial consultations from people without strong finances. I know people who consider themselves marital counselors, yet have terrible marriages, so you have to be vigilant. Other than excellent and confidential counsel, no one else should be privy to your marriage.

I'm so thankful for my spouse. I'm grateful for the way we practice love. We don't yell at each other because no meaningful solutions will come to us during a shouting match. We don't curse at each other because no love can be found in those words. It is hard to control the wild and duplicitous nature of the tongue, but it must be done. It doesn't mean that you can't yell, curse and be married for 50 years. That's just not the way we spend our time in our marriage. While we were dating, we practiced the same principles because we wanted to reap a loving and fruitful marriage. When people or organizations ask for my time, my decision to accept is weighed against the time I could be spending peacefully with the love of my life. If it can result in sowing something better for us, it may prove to be worth its weight, but it's a decision that we usually make together. I say, "usually" because there is always room to improve.

I wasn't raised around healthy marriages or many marriages at all. I didn't see many healthy relationships of any kind until I met the parents of my friends. I remember when my parents got married, the many years they spent debating divorce, and when they decided to finalize the divorce, though they remained friends. What I was originally exposed to, whether in my household, elsewhere in my family, or my community, was not what I wanted for myself. I remember saying that I wanted to get married before having children, and the response to me was a curt, "You never know what's going to happen." I'm so glad I didn't let that person's mindset ruin mine. I'd seen too many mothers (and some fathers) struggle to raise children on their own. This wasn't because their partner or spouse passed away or became ill or somehow unable to support though they wanted to, but because they brought a child into an unhealthy relationship. Poverty doesn't make a relationship unhealthy or poor, actions do. Many rich people have unhealthy marriages, and I wouldn't consider them to be fully wealthy in life. The person you lay your head next to matters. The person you are yoked with matters in how far you will go.

The one thing my spouse and I recommend to people who are dating is to travel together. You need to get in a situation that is supposed to be good, but where many things can go wrong. Pay attention to how that person treats people: the servers, greeters, bellhops, flight attendants, conductors and everyone you come across. How does this person respond to sudden conflict? Traveling is similar to life in that it is a journey, but most people focus solely on the destination. If you neglect the journey, your destination will not be as sweet. If you have a poor meal before the journey, sit in the worst seats on the plane/train/bus, and barely sleep, your journey will be difficult. Irritability is more likely, and disagreement can brew from minor nuisances. If you spend your journey arguing, or rushing to the destination, you'll be worn out upon arrival. Treat your journey as good as your destination. Whenever my spouse and I travel, we start a day early, and get a hotel where we live, but near the airport. We arrange transportation in advance or make sure the hotel has airport transportation, so we don't have to worry about it. We spend our time in the hotel hanging out, and if it's near a popular district, we may go out on the town. Depending on the occasion, we may contact the hotel or have our concierge arrange something special for us in our room. Regardless, the occasion is wonderful because we're preparing for another adventure together. We joke and laugh. We don't take ourselves too seriously. There have been times when we absolutely should've missed our flight, but we didn't stress, and we made it.

Being level-headed allows us to think clearly and solve problems as they arise, instead of debating over whether one of us caused it. We can prevent things from happening again after we've solved the problem. The solution will often reveal what went wrong and we can adjust accordingly. Because my spouse doesn't enjoy the process of traveling, I worked with him to figure out a way to make the process feel less like a task. We used money as a tool. Starting a day early at a great hotel makes the journey better. Having access to special lounges within the airport where we can bathe, get massages, eat and relax, make my spouse feel like he's somewhere other than a crowded airport. He can grab his noise-canceling headphones and get closer to enjoying himself.

When my friends and I travel together, we frequent the lounges as well. For those who hadn't previously been, it's a joy to watch them light up while being exposed to a new world. My mother enjoys the lounges as well. A great journey can strengthen and enhance any relationship. These are the little things that make the journey enjoyable, so the destination can be even more rewarding. The greatest thing about my journey is that I am blessed to spend it with the love of my life: Jibril A. Ikharo.

Here's some space for you to daydream about the person you love or would *want* to love:

Chapter 11: The End Game

"Sow your seed in the morning, and at evening let your hands not be idle, for you do not know which will succeed, whether this or that, or whether both will do equally well." - Ecclesiastes 11:6

This is a vital verse in scripture, and in life, whether you believe or not. If you put all of your work into your one job, all of your resources in one venture, only plant one seed or put all of your eggs in one basket, if something goes wrong with that one route, you'll be left with nothing. Never stop planting! We must have options because we don't know what the end will bring. Sowing in the morning requires preparation and prescience regarding the end game. Since we don't know which ventures or positions will bear the most fruit (or any fruit) in the end, sow multiple seeds, and don't stop sowing just because it's late in the game. Never be idle when you should be sowing. If you're not reaping, it's time to sow. After you reap, you can sow again.

Remember, that you will not reap what you did not sow. You will not get what you did not put in. If you want to reap oranges at the end, don't spend your time sowing apple seeds. If you don't sow towards financial literacy and financial freedom, you will not reap it. If you want to reap a healthy marriage, don't sow seeds of jealousy, pride, abuse, profanity or neglect. Sow understanding, patience, kindness, respect, and love. Always make the best of your time. I don't know how many people will buy this book, or how many people will be touched by it, but I know I have to sow it for it to have the chance to grow and thrive.

The differences between me as the rich sibling and my poor siblings are shown in the end game. I've never set out to sow without a plan for the end. In writing about exposure, vision, re-exposure, drive, and execution, the root of it is about sowing in the morning, all the way through the evening, and reaping in the end. Faith is involved because we don't know which seeds will be successful, though we want them all to be. This book is about differences in the way we spend our time, not our money. Producers spend time innovating, while consumers spend time looking for ways to spend. Who you are now, and what you have, are the results of how you've spent your time. If you want something different in the future, you must change the way you spend your time.

Getting rich and achieving wealth, is just like getting fit and staying fit. It takes consistent work. However, some people have it easier than others, while others just make it look easy. Don't think that because your friend seems to effortlessly grow wealth, work isn't involved. Also, don't be afraid to ask for, or pay for, guidance.

Your DNA is evidence that you're a survivor. The next level is thriving. Our ancestors have been through war, famine, disease, oppression, economic recessions, and so much more, but we are all here. They kept fighting for the end game. Don't let all of that striving and surviving end with you. Maybe there were some toxic practices and beliefs that survived as generations went on. Those things should stop with you. You may not be able to get your entire family to change unsavory attitudes or old habits, but you can change yourself. I believe that there was someone before me who believed the way that I do (or stronger) and had this passion (or far more), and that lives on through me. My wealth is from God but traveled through their seeds.

I spend my time sowing seeds of wealth in honor of our ancestors, and in honor of those to come.

Maura Ikharo, AICP

Picture Location: Brussels/Bruxelles, Belgium

Notes:

Notes:

Notes:

95